Altcoins Book Guide

A Comprehensive Manual on Investing in Alternative Cryptocurrencies

By
Ben Alexi

Copyright
All rights reserved and no part of this book may be reproduced or transmitted by any means or forms such as but not limited to: electronic, mechanical, photocopying, recording without the consent and written permission of the author/publisher first.

Legal Notice and Disclaimer
The information in this book Altcoins Book Guide and any materials that go along with it are only for informational purpose. It should not be by anyway legal, financial advice. The Publisher and author do not make any promise or guarantee from reading the Altcoins Book Guide. Please use your due diligence and research when investing in cryptocurrencies as the recommendations and suggestions in this book guide do not replace a legal advice on cryptocurrency investment.

The author had made every effort to ensure the accuracy of the information in the Altcoin book guide at the time when the book was written and published. The publisher or author does not assume any liability to any party for any disruption, loss, or damage being caused by unintentional, negligence, or accidental (or other cause) deletion, errors, or exclusion.

Table of contents

Introduction to Cryptocurrencies

CHAPTER ONE: Building a Crypto Portfolio

CHAPTER TWO: The Best Cryptocurrency Wallets

CHAPTER THREE: Alternative Cryptocurrencies to Consider

CHAPTER FOUR: Selecting the Best Cryptocurrency to Invest

CHAPTER FIVE: Less Obvious BUT Good Future Prospects

CHAPTER SIX: Tools Used to either Invest or Trade the Cryptocurrencies

CHAPTER SEVEN: Buying Cryptocurrencies

Conclusion

Other Books by the Author

Introduction to Cryptocurrencies

A successful business entails effective transaction between the buyers and the sellers. Both parties benefit from the introduction of the process. Ancient economists came up with the physical system of payment to validate the entire process.

However, the advancing technology forced the entrepreneurs to consider the online platforms since the studies indicated that most of their target customers spent most of their times in the internet.

To ensure that they conduct the process efficiently with the global market, there was need for a digital means of transaction that would convenience the business stakeholders. This digitalized commerce is both transparent and incorruptible.

Following the publication of the Satoshi Nakamoto's white paper in the year 2008, the idea of Bitcoin erupted to provide investment opportunities for the ambitious businesspeople. During the invention of this Bitcoin product, cryptocurrency emerged.

This electronic cash system uses the peer-to-peer network system to minimize the double spending during the transaction processes. The findings of this great inventor was a form of relief following the failure of all the centralized attempts. This decentralization of this cashless payment system prevents the incidences of forgery upon the confirmation of the transaction.

The revolutionary impacts of the cryptocurrencies brand the invention the "Dawn of a new economy" following the prediction that the global nations would focus on the cashless transactions within the respective regions to minimize the inconveniences that come with the physical transactional systems.

The fact that this payment system is free from manipulation preserves and increases its values over time with the media proving to be a fast and comfortable payment media across the globe. Their private and anonymous features allows it to be effective for the outlawed economic activities like the black market.

The global investors consider investing in this ecosystem of tokens and coins following its extreme volatility. Although the risk-takers risk losing their investments, the lucky ones have the ability to increase the value of the coins by up to 1000 percent within a week or two. Therefore, this high-tech invention uses the exchanges like the poloniex, shapeshift or the Okcoin to enhance the trade of hundreds of cryptocurrencies. The economic studies record that the volume of the coins exceeds the major European stock exchanges.

Although the Bitcoin remains to be the most famous cryptocurrency, the global users, including the investors keep their eyes on the several other cryptocurrencies to expand their investment opportunities. Among the cryptocurrencies, include the Riple, Ethereum, Waves, NEM, Dash and Monero.

Therefore, the later chapters of this book would provide information for the understanding of the alternative cryptocurrencies. This virtual monetary unit has no physical representation and is divisible into 100 million "Satoshis."

New Crypto investor need to build portfolios before opting to invest in the cryptocurrencies. However, it is hard for them to decide on the assets to include in the portfolio. Depending on the individual income, the risk takers can consider stating using a $119.673 portfolio. Using the small amount, the investors select the number of coins to invest depending on the specific desire of the investor.

Building a successful portfolio depends on the specific place to purchase the coin, the trading platform as well as selecting the safest coin to invest. However, despite considering all these factors, it is advisable for the investor to use the best apps to track his or her portfolio for determining the best protection of the investments.

To get started, therefore, simply buy a Bitcoin and send it to an exchange. The exchange is used to purchase the other coins you desire to invest in and make a fortune out of the trade.

Creating a cryptocurrency portfolio involves the crypto investors taking risks. The risk takers consider using the various formulas like the risk-reward formula to decide on the amount of risk they are comfortable with and this influences the specific coins they desire to invest in. Economists advise that the investors invest 50% of their capital on the safe-ish coins such as the Monero, Bitcoin or even the Erethereum. With the ever-increasing value of the coins, the entry point is very critical. The ambitious investors consider entering the trade when the coins are cheap. It is, therefore, advisable to consider purchasing the coins today due to the predicted increased values of the coins at the end of 2018 and years to come.

Conduct regular research to determine the trending and most valuable coins available in the market. Keeping the cryptocurrencies safe is another important aspect of the digital business.

The cryptocurrency wallets have outstanding features that make it convenience to safeguard our respective coins. The wallets ensures that the coins maintain their values upon the fluctuating economic conditions.

The many wallets available requires the investors to select the alternative that best suits their tastes. This selection requires prior assessment of the available options available in the market to ensure that the global investors do not lose their hard-earned cash.

Trezor, Coinbase, Nano Ledger S and KeepKey high-tech devices are some of the available wallets that could be helpful for the many ambitious people available across the globe, you included. Different tools also exist to help in the tracking of your progress as well as the latest prices and values of the gold coins.

Technical analysis and investing advice as well as the live prices and news available online are some of the tools that the goal-oriented persons consider in ensuring their investment in the cryptocurrency yields.

The information collected include the latest crypto news such as the historical price data and the latest market prices. However, despite the commercial benefits that come with the digital coins, investing in the cryptocurrencies exposes the investors to losses.

Therefore, it is critical to understand both the negative and positive outcomes of considering this form of e-commerce before opting to invest in the trending gold coins.

Therefore, the later chapters of this book not only explain the reasons why and why not to invest in this form of business but also the criteria to use while considering the best coin for your investments.

You, therefore, need to consider going through this book to ensure that you understand all the aspects of this investment to be sure of securing your hard-earned resources for a valuable experience in this form of online business.

CHAPTER ONE: Building a Crypto Portfolio

Global investors consider diversifying their investments across many different classes of assets to minimize their exposure to risks. The reduced risk means that the entrepreneurs realize many returns out of their investment.

However, creating a successful and long-term portfolio is critical and involves a series of steps that need to be followed systematically. The global users decide to build either a long-term or a dynamic portfolio depending on their desires. Whereas the long-term portfolio resembles the retirement portfolio, the dynamic portfolio enables the user to continue trading the cryptocurrencies as they wish.

This chapter, therefore, entails the explanation of the specific steps involved in setting up a successful cryptocurrency portfolio for a memorable experience throughout the investment process. Before considering investing in the best cryptocurrencies, it is advisable to determine the amount you are willing to risk first. For this reason, the economists advise that the investors should not risk more than they can afford.

Once you have decided the amount to put into the investment, the next step is figure out a diversification plan that entails spreading across all the top 5 or 10 of the top cryptocurrencies in the global market.

This consideration protects you from the coins with the plenty of trading volumes or popularity automatically. Other than the secured protection, this diversification allows the risk taker to get to understand the entire cryptocurrency market.

This understanding enhances the experience of the veteran investors to realize many returns throughout their time risking their hard-earned cash. Depending on the success of the selected coins, the user adjusts his or her holdings accordingly. Three building blocks (research, position sizing and entry price) leads to the efficient portfolio entry.

1. Research

Crypto world entails all sorts of exciting and confusing elements that the investor needs to understand before staking their resources. Research is, therefore, a key concept in the cryptocurrency investment. It not only allows the gamblers to identify the best coins to risk their resources but also the payment methods for the cryptocurrencies as well as the best wallet to consider. This pre-assessment is critical for the ambitious members of the globe to make fortunes out of their investments.

There exist many online platforms to allow the users to conduct their studies on the wise economic moves for the benefits of the digitalized population. Analyzing the coins entails identifying their specific founders of the respective coins.

Understanding how the blockchain technology works as well as the specific strategies to set up a wallet is essential before opting to set up a portfolio for an enhanced online commerce. Although following the various publications regarding how effective to build your cryptocurrency portfolio for maximum output out of the whole process.

2. Position sizing

The main intention of conducting the comprehensive research regarding the current market condition is to ensure that you make sound decisions, including the profitable coins as well as the most appropriate time to buy the coins to invest in them for a profitable return.

The findings from the useful study follows the making of decision on the next step to take. Now that you have the facts about the market and the best coin to consider, it is the time to decide on the amount of resources to invest into the selected coin with the aim of making huge returns. The successful investors use many of their resources to invest in the coins they believe will expose them to less risks compared to the available options.

To ensure that you make the best decision in selecting the best profitable coins, the experienced in this type of business consider attaching either the Low, Medium or the High rating against each of the coins and try rationalizing the position sizing.

Every rating represents a specific percentage of your total investment. Ou of the displayed percentage, you are the one to decide the percentage you feel comfortable with. Because of the lacking clues about the risk you are exposing yourself to, the professionals advise the investors to put a little percentage of their hard-earned cash. The fluctuating coin prices also makes it challenging for the goal-oriented depositors in determining the risk level of their decisions. In case you desire to invest 10 percent of your resources, for example, it would be wise to invest only five percent and leave the remaining the portion for future investment. This minimizes the chances of the inventors to realize many losses as a result.

The prices of the coins will continue going up and down hence the need to be flexible even upon creating your successful portfolio. The regular manipulation of the platforms will help you to realize maximum outcome of your wise decision and move regarding the respective gold coins to put your resources.

3. The entry point

Upon the identification of the coin to invest in as well as the time and amount to put into action, the entry point is so critical for the success of the business. Despite being sure that your selected gold coin will make you a fortune, the professional economist that specialize in this form of business claim that it is not wise to put all your resources on them.

The fact that the prices of the coins fluctuate means that you risk experiencing losses even with the most preferred coin. Within a span of months, for example, a Bitcoin-USD graph experiences crazy runs ups, including the significant corrections and the slight recovery phases.

This finding means that the entry point or the time you decide to invest on the coin is critical in predicting the expected returns out of the passionate moves.

There is significant difference between buying the coins while in a dip and when at the top hence the need to employ your technical skills, including the critical analysis of the historic resistance and the support levels before making your prediction regarding the prices of the coin in the future.

The need to make your personal conclusion results following the fact that the inadequate history regarding the resistance and support levels. However, this prediction criterion is not essential in case you are here for a sort-term adventure. The historic analysis also allows you to determine whether the trading of the coins are subjects of a lot of volatility or not. Upon the decision to make your investment, you will need to determine the best wallet to keep your buy safe. The next chapter, therefore, includes the various wallets that would be useful for you.

CHAPTER TWO: The Best Cryptocurrency Wallets

A digital wallet is critical in ensuring the efficient transfer of the digital currency as well as monitoring their balance. The software program store both the private and public keys that enhances the interaction with the various blockchain to facilitate their functionalities.

Unlike the traditional wallet, the cryptocurrency wallet does not store the currency in a specific location in any physical form, but the records of transactions. This program allows you to monitor your balance, sending money as well as regulating the other operations that signifies the blockchain technology.

The system operates in that an individual that sends you the gold coins signs off his or her ownership of the coin to your wallet's address. However, to use the digital coins and unlock the funds, your private key need to match the public address assigned to the currency.

Many wallets are available to give you the opportunity to select the one that best suits your taste. This section of the book, therefore, provides you with the explanation of the common wallets that are available for you to choose from, including how the digital market works to facilitate your experience with the gold coins.

Once the public and private keys match, the balance within your digital market increases while the senders decrease accordingly. Although the program does not allow the transaction of real coins, the transaction record on the blockchain as well as the changes in the balance in your cryptocurrency wallet signifies the operation.

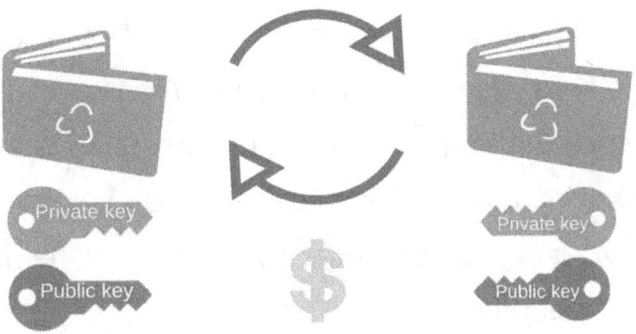

The private and public key need to match to facilitate the process.

Many wallets help in the storage and accessibility of your digital currencies. The wallets, however, can be divided into three hardware, software and paper, with the wallets can be a desktop, online or mobile:

Desktop: the wallets are downloaded an installed on a laptop or PC. However, you can only access the wallet from a single computer on which the digital wallet is downloaded and installed. This type of wallet offer one of the top security features for your cryptocurrency. Problem arise when the computer is hacked or rather is infected with the virus. In such a scenario, you risk losing your funds.

Online: unlike the desktop wallet types, these wallet that run on the cloud are accessible from any computing devise regardless of the location. The private keys are stored online and controlled by the third party that makes them more vulnerable to theft and hacking attacks. Despite the challenges that face these wallets, they are more convenient for the users that consider them.

Hardware: other than in the case of the online and software wallets, these wallets store your private keys on hardware devices such as the USB. Despite having an offline storage platform, the transactions are done online hence increased security.

Another advantage of this type of wallets is that they are compatible with several web interfaces that can support the different currencies depending on your preferred coins. To facilitate its functionality, the user simply needs to connect the device to any available internet-enabled computer then key in a security pin before opting to send currency.

The process is completed by confirming the operation. In addition to enhancing an easy transaction, the hardware also allows you to keep your money offline and away from danger.

Paper: this type of wallet allows provides high security option for your currencies. This form of digital wallet entails a software that securely generates a pair of keys before they are printed out. The transfer of your gold coin to your paper wallet is straightforward.

The transfer of the Bitcoin is accomplished through the transfer of the funds from your preferred software wallet to the public address displayed on your paper wallet. In case you desire to withdraw or rather spend the currencies, however, simply transfer your fund from the paper wallet to the software wallet. This "sweeping" process can either be done manually through the keying in of your private keys or automatically through scanning the QR code on your paper wallet.

Some of the best wallets cryptocurrency wallets to consider.

There are many different wallets categorized into the above types. The wallets help in monitoring your online transactions to ensure that you minimize the risk of making losses out of your investments on the gold coins.

Despite the distinctive features that make the wallets unique, some specific desirable traits that the entire crypto wallet need to have:

- ✓ The cost of the of using the wallet need to be affordable and with minimum drawbacks
- ✓ Determine whether the company dealing with your selected wallet has a history of security issues.
- ✓ The accessibility of the wallet is critical for the selection of your best alternative.

- ✓ He wallet need to be convenient for the users with regard to its speed to purchase any currency.
- ✓ The wallets need to user-friendly
- ✓ The designs need to meet the diverse global users.

For this reason, the professional economists argue recommend the wallet that offers all the above-mentioned characteristics for an enhanced experience in this online business.

A. Trezor Wallet

This hardware wallet is designed to work with nearly all the operating systems. The cryptocurrency wallet supports the Bitcoin, DASH, Zcsh, Ethereum Classc, Bitcoin Cash, Expanse, UBIQ, Ethereum among the other ERC 20 tokens.

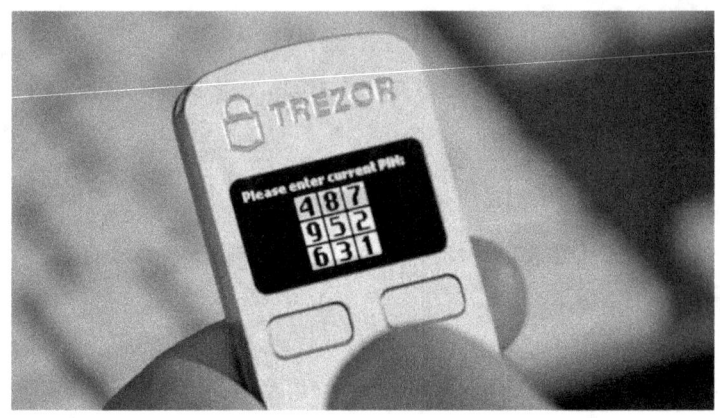

Trezor Wallet

B. Ledger Nano

This cryptocurrency wallet is similar to the Trezor Wallet. The hardware wallet supports multiple cryptocurrencies. The users of this wallet have the ability of physically approving their transactions by simply pushing the buttons on the device before the execution of the transactions.

This second security layer eliminates the sudden attacks that might undermine the success of the transactions. The users that prefer this wallet consider dealing with the Ripple, Qutum, NEO, PIVX, Vertcoin, Viacoin, Zcash, Litecoin, Komodo, Hcash, Digibyte, Bcash, Dash,Ark, Bitcoin Gold, Bitcoin, Stellar, S

Tratis, Starts as well as the Ubiq.

The Ledger Nano S Cryptocurrency Wallet

C. Exodus Wallet

This Exodus wallet is a software wallet that is available for personal computers. This wallet has the ShapeShift utility built into it to makes it easy for the conversion or purchasing of a cryptocurrency with another without the user having to leave the wallet interface.

This wallet supports the BAT, Bitcoin, Aragon, Augur, Dash, Civic, EOS, Ethereum ETH Classic, Gnosis,

FunFair, SALT, Litecoin, OmiseGo, Golem, Distric0x as well as the Decred coins.

The Exodus Wallet

D. Coinomi Wallet

This wallet is a mobile multi-currency cryptocurrency that is compatible only with the Android operating system. Unlike the other cryptocurrencies wallets, this program supports a wide range of cryptocurrency assets such as the People, Feathercoin, Game Credits, NuShares, OKCash, Peercoin, POSW, Putincoin, Egulden among several other coins. The company dealing with the wallets are working hard to introduce the IOS version in the years to come.

The Coinomi Wallet

E. Jaxx Wallet

Professionals argue that this one of the digital wallet that supports the multi-currencies. This product of the Decentral Company supports the Ether Classic, Dash, Ether, DAO, REP, Bitcoin and the Litecoin cryptocurrencies. Unlike the Coinomic wallet that only conforms with the android operating system, the user of this wallet have the ability to download it for both the desktop or mobile devices such as the Androids, iPad, MAC, Google Chrome browser extension, Linux, Windows as well as the Tablets.

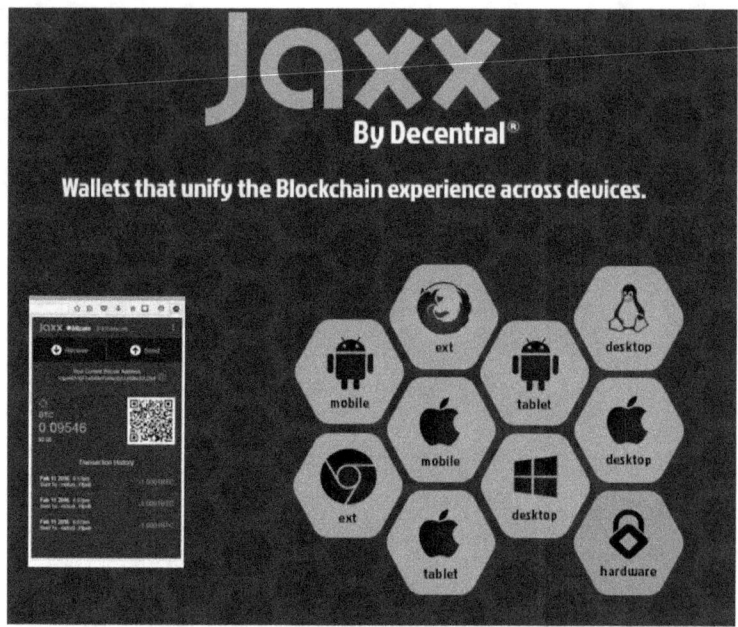

The Jaxx Wallet

F. The Agama Wallet

Although it is still in the development stage, the Agama Wallet offers unique feature that allows the users to use the multiple cryptocurrencies as well as choosing the security they feel is best for them. This wallet supports the Bitcoin Dark, Franko, Litecoin, Unocoin, Zcash, Dogecoin, DigiByte, Carbocoin, Komodo, Zetacoin, Game Credit as well as the Bitcoin cryptocurrencies. Unfortunately, this wallet is only available for the desktops. Economists believe that the mobile-supported versions are yet to come.

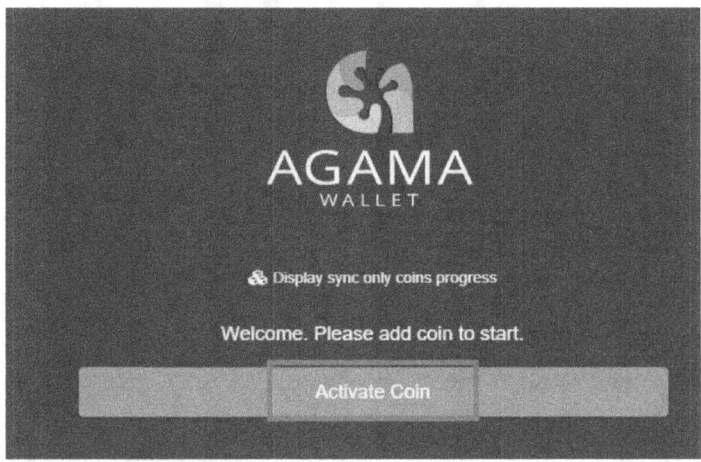

The Agama Wallet

In addition to the above mentioned wallets, there are other wallets that can also prove to be essential for a memorable experience when dealing with the coins. These include the Blockchain.info (an online wallet), Coinbase (online exchange), MyEtherWallet (paper wallet) and the Electrum (a software wallet).

It is, therefore, important to conduct comprehensive research regarding the best wallet to consider for what cryptocurrency before you decide to acquire either of them.

Are The Cryptocurrency Wallets Reliable?

The available wallets are secure to varying degrees, with the level of security depending on the type of wallet one decide to use as well as the service providers. Recent studies indicate that the web servers are intrinsically riskier media compared to the offline option.

However, despite the fact that the online wallets prove to be the most vulnerable, there are specific precautions that when taken minimize the exposure of the user to the risk of losing their hard-earned resources:

I. Update your software regularly

Keeping your software up-to-date ensures that you have access to the latest security enhancement. In addition to the wallet software, you are required to update also the software available on your mobile or computer.

II. Backup your wallet

Keep a vast majority of your funds in a high security environment, with only a small amount of the currency for everyday application stored either online, on your mobile or computer. Either the offline or cold storage alternatives are available for the backups like the paper, USB or Ledger Nano help in protecting you against computer failures as well as the chance to recover your wallet once it is stolen or accessed by the hackers.

III.   Add the extra security layers

Experienced users claim that the more security layer you consider the better. Setting up of passwords, for example, protects the accessibility of your funds by the unauthorized persons. For the security issues, consider the wallets that offer the multisig transactions such as the Copay or Armory. Such trades require permission of another user before it is completed.

CHAPTER THREE:

Alternative Cryptocurrencies to Consider

Cryptocurrency has become a hot topic with regard to online businesses. The rise of Bitcoin above $10,000 proves the viability of the digital markets. Bitcoin market was worth $250 billion with the value expected to rise even higher.

However, cryptocurrency is more than just the Bitcoin. More than 1,500 currencies were in circulation by April 2018 indicating a market of about $330 billion. The best news is that some of these of altcoins are designed to handle more transactions that Bitcoin can do, with others designed to enhance the user security, for example.

The problem comes in selecting the best alternative for the Bitcoin. This chapter, therefore, not only includes the common altcoins but also the steps involved in evaluating whether the alternative cryptocurrency is worth the investment.

Bitcoins

Evaluating the best coin to consider for your business is critical in ensuring that you make the best decisions in terms of choosing the cryptocurrency that would continue enhancing the success of the digital market. This assessment considers a series of factors that would help you in determining the alternative cryptocurrency to Bitcoin:

i. **Development activity**

One way through which the successful crypto investors make a fortune out of their operation is reviewing the development activity of every cryptocurrency. The goal-oriented people claim that a team that push out updates as well as patch the bugs at all times is the best company to consider buying their product.

Recent studies indicate that Bitcoin has the most active development team, with all its work done publicly through the Github repository making it open for anyone to check if any of the developers is not playing his or her part.

The fact that all the altcoins are products of the Bitcoins calls for the need for regular updates in case of a bug found in the Bitcoin. This move follows the fact that the bug will certainly affect the altcoin because of the fact that they share similar codebase. It is, therefore, important to select the alternative cryptocurrency that provides more updates to enhance the users' experience.

ii. **The technical and monetary rules innovation**

Although the limited creation of the Bitcoin at about 21 million coins contributes to its increased value, some people see this as a limiting factor. Alternative coins such as the Dogecoin that has about 100 billion coins and with no hard cap is expected to grow by 5.256

billion coins every year once it hits the 100 billion mark.

This change of monetary rules, unlike in the case of the Bitcoin, motivates the investors to consider the altcoins. Different cryptocurrencies have use the diverse innovations to benefit the overall ecosystem hence good evaluating criteria for the altcoins.

iii. **Public interest**

The popularity of the coin is critical for the selection of the alternative cryptocurrency to invest in. To do this, simply quick search the name of the coin on Bing or Google and the number of results that exist regarding the coin would represent its popularity. Established coins will have millions of search results. You can also determine how popular a coin's official website on Alexa.

iv. **Market capitalization**

The coins with the low market capitalization are prone to manipulation hence the development of scam coins. Considering such altcoins would expose you to the risk of losing a lot of money. On the other hand, the coins that enjoy the larger market capitalization will be harder to manipulate since it would require a significantly larger capital base to influence the prices.

v. Community strength

The coins that lack a community is not valuable since no one will opt to use the coin. Although it is difficult to determine the number of users for a specific coin due to its decentralized nature, you can use proxies to estimate the size of the community. The Facebook likes, Reddit activity and Twitter followers are the examples of the proxies used.

vi. The trading liquidity and volume

A trading activity surrounding an altcoin is essential in determining whether to buy it. You, therefore, need to purchase the alternative cryptocurrencies that many users trading it.

The More Obvious and Solid Altcoins to Invest In

There are many different alternatives to Bitcoin. Therefore, the following are some of the common or obvious coins that are valuable for the crypto investors:

1) Ethereum

This coin, first proposed by Vitalik Buterin (a Russian programmer) in the late 2013, adds to the Blockchain technology. This cryptocurrency enables smart contracts to be written, with the trades subjects to conditions. This coin is currently trading at above $500 and is expected to appreciate as years go. Analysts rank this altcoin second after Bitcoin.

The Ethereum altcoin

2) Ripple

With the market value at $26.3 billion, this altcoin was designed in the yer 2012 to help in settling trade rather than the creating a trading frenzy. About 38 billion Ripples are in circulation currently, with its value remaining relatively stable as commodities are moved across the water bodies. Unlike the other currencies, Ripple is distributed by the creators of the coin, ripple Labs of San Francisco.

The Ripple Altcoins

3) Bitcoin Cash

This cryptocurrency came into existence in August 2017 as a means to solve the costly and onerous transactions that burdened the Bitcoin users. The market value of this coin is at $12.9 billion. Bitcoin Cash has the same mining procedure as the Bitcoin.

The Bitcoin Cash

4) Litecoin

This coin also referred as a "silver to Bitcoin's gold" has a market value of about $7.3 billion. This cryptocurrency is a decentralized network designed to handle the trades as fast as possible.

The Litecoin updates its blockchain more often that the Bitcoin hence allowing the use of its Scrypt algorithm to mine on the PCs rather the expensive graphic systems required for the Bitcoin.

Analysts claim that the price of this altcoin mirrors that of the Bitcoin.

The Litecoin

5) Dash

This coin was introduced in the year 2014 as an XCoin based on the Bitcoin technology, with a market value of about $3.0 billion.

This coin uses its own blockchain and mining system. The cryptocurrency offers features for both the instant transactions known as InstantSend and the private transaction called PrivateSend. The two properties are enabled because of both the "nodes" and the larger "masternodes."

The Dash Altcoin

There are many altcoins to choose from and hence there is need to engage yourself in comprehensive research to determine the best alternative cryptocurrency to place your hard-earned cash.

CHAPTER FOUR: Selecting the Best Cryptocurrency to Invest In

Economics analysts predict that the interest for the cryptocurrencies will continue to grow, with the value for the individual coins expected to increase in years to come. This prediction is based on the current indices showing how the crypto investment outperforms all the hedge fund investments in the stocks.

However, the fact that there are many different coins calls for the research studies on the respective gold coins with the primary intention of deciding on the best cryptocurrency you would desire to invest in. for this reason, this chapter includes the crucial aspects that need to be considered in selecting the best coins to invest in.

You need to determine the exact problems that the gold coin intends to solve before buying and investing in it. This consideration depends on whether the cryptocurrency has long-term value or not depending on the desires of the users. You need to have a clear vision for considering the coins.

Professional economists advise the crypto investors to consider purchasing the coins that have real-world value. The world-focused cryptocurrencies are more valuable and hence the visionary investors should consider them for positive returns.

The companies dealing with your selected coins need to have a long-term vision for the currencies to be sure that you enjoy their values for a prolonged period hence increased profit rates.

In addition to the development team commitment, you also need to review some of the users' comments regarding the coins to give you a hint on what to expect from investing in your preferred coin.

Having such knowledge gives you the power to predict the coins that will be valuable in years to come and those that you expect to lose their values.

The competition between the coins determines the best one to invest in. analysis of this aspect is critical following the existence of coins that help in solving similar problems.

Experienced investors claim that it is not wise to choose a coin to help solve an issue without considering the others that serve the same purpose. You, therefore, need to visit the respective websites of the coins to be determine whether it looks professional or rather makes sense.

Critically research on the potential security issues that either coin is exposed to. Above all, it is advisable to try whether the software of either coin works effectively to avoid inconveniences in the future.

Considering all these aspects will help you determine the best option to consider while trying solving the global issues that undermine the livelihood of those residing in the jurisdiction.

The float and maximum supply determines the best cryptocurrency to consider for investment. This consideration is favorable for the users who are in for a long-term cryptocurrency investments.

The Bitcoin, for example, can only have about 21 million coins created hence determining its demand and supply.

Once all the coins are mined, the supply will decrease while the demand increases hence determining the price rates. On the other hand, the 100 million Ripple coins make the price of the coin to remain relatively low.

The same amount of Ether will be produced every year ensuring an unlimited supply hence lowering its prices further. The relationship between the demand and supply for the respective coins determines their value with the Bitcoin being the most valuable of all the coins.

The purchase availability for the individual cryptocurrencies is a special factor in selecting the specific coin to invest in. the currency that is available on the big exchanges to allow many people access it has more potential to experience an increase in value.

The fact that a currency is hard to get is not enough to rule it out of your selection. You are free to consider whichever coin you like following a comprehensive research. The availability of the respective coins is also an essential factor that the successful investors consider in selecting the best coins to invest in.

New users, on the same note, need to consider this aspect as a route to a successful business intervention. In addition to the availability of the currencies, the storage options for the respective coins is another criterion for determining the success of the investment. The experienced investors consider the ease of storage when selecting the best coin to risk their hard-earned resources. The preferred wallet options need to be easy to use for your convenience.

Marketing is another factor that determines the success of the currencies. Although the cryptocurrencies are decentralized and are community owned, there is still the need for marketing just the same way the Apple Company continue marketing their high-quality products.

Studies indicate that there are many excellent ideas that did not materialize to enhance the existence of the global population following the bad marketing strategies the founders employed. With regard to this, you need to consider the cryptocurrency whose development team are determined to market it.

To determine this, it is advisable to visit their social media channels, including their Twitter account to be sure of their commitment to expanding their customer clouds. You also need to consider the role of the online influencers in promoting the currencies you desire to invest in. it is, therefore, crucial to assess the marketing of the individual currencies since the economists claim that their success depends on excellent marketing interventions.

Unfortunately, numerous cases of scam coins have been reported since the introduction of this form of business. However, it is required that you consider the following option to minimize the chances of being the victim of this fraudulent operation:

- Have a confirmed information about the person that is behind the coin you desire to purchase. You need to select the coins whose development team comprises of known members of the cryptocurrency community.
- Be sure of the type of escrow that holds the coins for their customers until they complete a set deal during the transaction.
- Do not consider the projects that lack any link to the code.
- Be careful with the projects that make bold claims about their products. Avoid the cryptocurrencies with small market capitalization or those with low trading volumes.

It is, therefore, important that you conduct a lot of research to identify the currencies that are valuable while at the same time avoid the swindle coins.

CHAPTER FIVE: Less Obvious BUT Good Future Prospects

Chapter three of this book explains some of the common and trending alternative crptocurrencies that a new crypto investor can choose from. The altcoins mentioned are thought to be the best alternative for the Bitcoin, which is the most valuable of all according to the experienced crypto investors who have realizd huge returns out of their investments.

In addition, new users who decided to risk on the coins have affirmed that the above mentioned cryptocurrencies have made their endeavors successful.

Other than the above mentioned altcoins, there exist other gold coins that are not known by many. Assessment of the values of these coins shows that investing in them is a wise decision to make.

This chapter, therefore, explains ten less obvious altcoins, including the reason why to invest in them for a fruitful future.

1. **The ARK Altcoin**

The ARK altcoin is storming the crypto market following its sudden increase in value. By 23 January 2018, this gold coin recorded the third highest crypto price having increased by 19.28% in a span of 24 hours.

This altcoin is an all-in –one blockchain solution, with te user only needing the "Point. Click. Blockchain" to enjoy a more innovative blockchain technology.

The altcoin's wallet supports all the major operating systems both on the desktops and the Android and iOS mobile devices. This gold coin uses the Delegated-Proof-of-Stake (DPoS) consensus mechanism made of up to 51 delegates spread worldwide, with the aim of running the ARK network for a block reward. This strategy aims at multiplying the number of users.

In addition to the dependency on the DPoS mechanism, the ARK team is striving to integrate multiple programming languages into the system to be sure that many developers consider using the ARK.

Unfortunately, the value o the altcoin is declining, with the ranking moving down to 49th position. However, despite the prediction that the crisi will continue in years to come, the transparent and determined ARK team make it a worthwhile project to consider. This advantage that the ARK has over the other alternative cryptocurrencies confirms the ARK's Reddit forum that surpassed the 20,000 subscribers recently. The diehards of this altcoin give its SmartBridge system as the most attractive feature that might boost the altcoin.

Ark (ARK)

The ARK altcoins

2. The NEO Altcoin

The NEO altcoin is one of the blockchain platforms that facilitates the development of the smart contracts and the digital assets similar to the Ethereum, this platform uses two different tokens: Gas and the NEO to enhance the experience of the investors.

The NEO team claim that the main objective of the project is to use the smart contracts to provide a decentralized and well-distributed platform for the non-digital assets. you will be able to pay your rent using the smart contract automatically every month other than setting up a bank account.

Therefore, this China's response to Ethereum aims at bridging the gap between the traditional and digital assets.

Following its appearance in the year 2016, the altcoin ranked 20th, therefore, achieving a $5billion market capitalization by the end of the next year (2017). However, the American economic research studies predict the value of the NEO market to grow at a rate of 32% by the year 2023. One of the success of the NEO cryptocurrency is the media attention.

The prices of the coin was driven by the headlines. Just like both the Dash and Monero, NEO is fairly resistant to regulations since the developers openly state their willingness to work with the authorities.

The NEO altcoin

3. The OmiseGO cryptocurrency

The developers of the OmiseGO project built it on the Ethereum platform back in the year 2013. This OmiseGO is more than an altcoin, with it rather offering the users with the alternative to enhance their online exchanges.

This project connects the existing cryptocurrency wallets to the central OmiseGO blockchain to substitute the traditional buying and selling of the gold coins from the exchanges. The open payment platform uses the "Unbank the Banked" slogan with the main objective being to provide better financial services for the global population, including both the people that utilize the traditional banking and those that lack the traditional infrastructures, especially in the developing nations.

Currently, the cryptocurrency ranks at 19th with a market capitalization of about $1,506,964,404 and valued at $14.77 this year (2018), with the experts predicting it to maintain an upward trend in terms of its value.

The OmiseGO Altcoin

4. The IOTA Altcoin

Unlike the other coins built on the Blockchain technology, the IOTA cryptocurrency is a product of the Tangle technology. This technology aims at responding to the issues with scalability, security and fees. Unfortunately, the financial institutions are unable to use this Tangle as the base technology following its inability of having the time dependent Transactions.

This cryptocurrency listed as MIOTA on exchanges is all about the Internet of Things, with the consumers using the connected devices more and more.

The IOA desires to be the cryptocurrency that supports the intended machine-to-machine transactions across the universe.

All the machine connected to the network acts as the nodes to verify the transactions, with the responsible team for tis development claiming that the coin is not on my tamper-proof but secure as well.

The IOTA Altcoin

5. The TenX Altcoin

This digital coin provides the user with the ability to spend the cryptocurrencies anytime they desire using a debit card linked to a mobile application. The project aimed at connect the the virtual and physical platforms on the existing infrastructure, which the growing numbers of businesses and users struggle to leverage.

The investors of this digitalcoin own TenX Card (a debit card) that come with a TenX Wallet to allow them facilitate the payment processes. Currently, the cards can be used in about 200 countries, with approximately more than 36 million points of acceptance. The success is because of the partnership between the TenX team and the major credit card firms.

This project uses both the COMIT Routine Protocol and the Cross-chain Payment Channels to award the users with the ability to use the blockchain assets, making TenX to be the first liquidity provider to offer the real-world payments.

The TenX Card

6. The Neblio Altcoin

This digital coin is one of the cryptocurrencies with the market value of more than $150 million, with the market cap reading at around $176 million. This coin currently trades primarily on the Binance that accounts for about 97.3 percent its total volume.

Economic analysts advise the crypto investors to consider this coin because of the availability of Neblio Github that displays signs of strong and consistent development in case they desire to realiz huge returns of out of their investments.

Other than the release of the Electrum Lite Wallet, this project introduces an Android app, with a submitted Neblio iOS app for approval by the Apple Company. The success makes the program a boost for the digital community.

Neblio (NEBL)

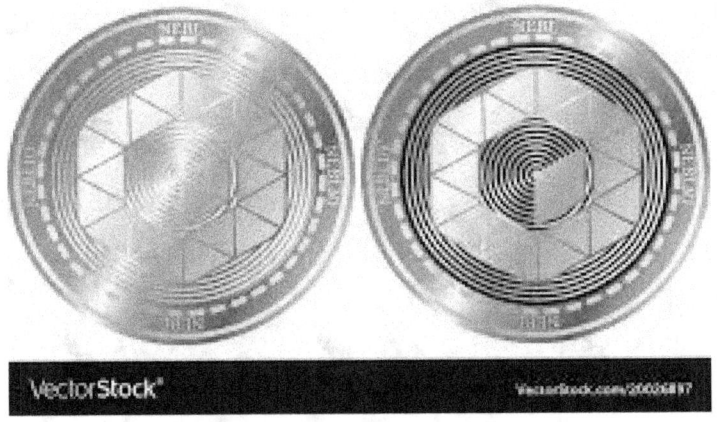

The Neblio Altcoin

7. The Steem Altcoin

This decentralized cryptocurrency runs on the Steem blockchain. This technology is also known for powering both the blogging platform and the Steemit social media. Unlike the Bitcoin or Ether, this digital coin is not mineable but the technology simply allocates the STEEM tokens into the reward funds used to pay the Steemit users for contributing to the platform.

The coin is also applicable in making the digital peer-to-peer payments. This 2016 release enjoys a market capitalization of about $1.5 billion ranking in the top 25 of the most valuable cryptocurrencies.

This product with a daily volume of approximately $50 million can be traded on the leading cryptocurrencies exchanges like the Poloniex and the Bittrex among others available.

Steem (STEEM)

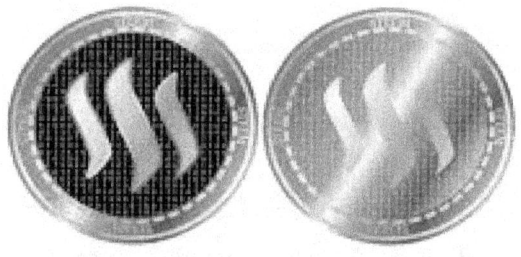

The Steem Altcoin

8. The Private Instant Verified Transaction (PIVX) Altcoin

This digital coin came into existence back in January 31 2016 as a product of the DASH coin, with the difference being the consensus method used for the

PIVX. Whereas the PIVX uses the Proof of Stake (PoS), DASH employees the Proof of Work (PoW).

The PIVX coin uses the zerocoin protocol to enhance its privacy features. Other than the enhanced privacy, the main goal of this coin is for an effective and fast exchange methods. Unfortunately, analysts claim that the coin is susceptible to criminal activities following its emphasis on the privacy.

However, this gold coin is highly volatile, experiencing massive increase in valuation and trading volumes. PIVX, in particular, has a market capitalization of about $191 million, with about $1 million traded daily. Another unique feature is the fact that it uses the light-weight Quark algorithm that works with little energy and memory space.

The PIVX Altcoin

9. The Loopring Altcoin

This open source decentralized exchange protocol enjoys a market capitalization of about $50 million, with the price per coin standing at around $0.65 to allow more room for future growth.

This growth possibility makes the coin the best for the crypto investors to consider. The technology behind the production of this product was to eliminate the counterparty risks, reducing the dependency on the centralized third parties as well as improving liquidity through an order pooling mechanism.

By September 2017, this gold coin expressed a volatile chart pattern on Binance to be at $0.055 (indicating a small growth rate). In addition, the product works as a public set of smart contracts that are responsible for settlement and trade.

This release is different from the other decentralized exchange protocols due to its ability to mix-and-match the orders, including the dissimilar orders hence improving liquidity. Therefore, the loopring solution uses the open smart contracts as well as the unique array of decentralized actors hence fulfilling the different functions in the looping system.

Loopring (LRC)

The Loopring Altcoins

10. The NULS Altcoins

This customizable blockchain is essential for both the long-term and short-term investors. NULS altcoin divides the blockchain into several modules network, storage, account, consensus, smart contract and ledger to enhance its reliability.

This coin provides the smart contract, cross-chain consensus as well as the multi-chain mechanism. The release of this coin promotes the usage of blockchain technology in the commercial world.

Economists argue that it is advisable to consider investing in this digital coin following its market capitalization of only $55 million, which means that it is a promising coin. The crypto investors who are hungry for more income consider purchasing this coin to make a fortune out of it.

The NULS logo

In addition to the ten coins explained in this chapter, there are several other coins not known by many but have proven to be the best investment platform for the ambitious digital investors.

Therefore, depending on whether you are in for a long-term or short-term level, you need to conduct comprehensive research studies to select the best digital coin that would make you a fortune.

CHAPTER SIX: Tools Used to either Invest or Trade the Cryptocurrencies

The Blockchain technology provides opportunities for the fortunate investors to make millions out of their time on the internet. Economists claim that the successful companies simply began with an idea before storming to be the source of billions for the respective stakeholders.

This technology allows the crypto investors to make huge fortune following their decision to invest in the trending cryptocurrencies.

In addition to the tools that help you identify the latest and best cryptocurrencies, other tools can help you keep track of the cryptocurrency portfolio following the new records set by the Bitcoin price nearly every week.

This chapter, therefore, explains the various tools that can help the new users, including you to make sound decisions while dealing with the different gold coins with the aim of making a fortune.

Therefore, you are required to conduct significant researches before downloading and installing the most favorable apps that would help you in managing your crypto business throughout the entire season.

a. CoinGecko

Although it is still in the biometric evaluation and (BEAT) testing, this tool prove to be a priceless tool for the cryptocurrency traders as well as the investors who desire to be competitive for the limited market available.

This platform ranks the cryptocurrencies across the multiple exchanges to enable you to have a glance into your preferred cryptocurrency, its real-time price as well as the percentage gain or decline during the transaction session.

The platform also displays the analyzed findings of the market cap of the different cryptocurrencies as well as the insight regarding the development and the community activity of the coin to prove the fact that the respective developers are still backing the stock.

The community activities also showed how the respective cryptocurrencies enjoyed a strong community of users.

b. The cryptowatch

Although most of the tools are helpful in researching for the best gold coins or marketplace to acquire them, this cryptowatch option is helpful in the improvement of your trading success once you have already bought your desired cryptocurrency. This apparatus provides live feeds about hundreds of cryptocurrencies across all the eight different exchanges.

The investors from the different parts of the world view the cryptowatch's live feeds that tracks the cryptocurrencies across the global currencies. This advantage enables them to make a selection of the coins based on the stack against their respective currencies.

Considering this tool is, therefore, critical in predicting the outcome of your investments on the coins of your choice.

c. The cryptofolio app

This application is helpful for the investors to monitor their cryptocurrencies, equities as well as their investments. The tool gives regular reports on your portfolio hence convenient for the users. There are two accounts plans for this tool: the free version for the new comers as well as the premium account for those who would wish to explore the significance of this cryptofolio.

> Comment [AM]: Specialize I tracking

The users of the premium accounts enjoy extra features that the free account owners cannot. However, not all the premium features are necessary for every crypto trader or investor.

Unfortunately, the users that desire to access the premium option have to pay an annual fee of approximately $240 currently, with the figure being subject to fluctuation as years count.

The cryptofolio accepts the payment of the valuable coins like the Bitcoin and the Litecoin. In case you are a lover of the notifications and the technical solutions as well as a more tracked account, it is advisable to download and install this application on your device for proper management of your hard-earned cash.

d. Cointracking

This company specializes in tracking both the profits and losses from your portfolio to help you make relevant adjustments to maximize on the profits while minimizing the negative returns. This free-to-use tool is available in both the desktop and web versions to make it convenient for the diverse users.

e. TabTrader

The users of the mobile cryptocurrency portfolio can enjoy this tool to manage their investments. This TabTrader mobile application supports a dozen of exchanges in the current days.

Unfortunately, some of the foreign and smaller exchanges are not accessible when you consider using this apparatus. Although this tool works perfectly on the mobile devices, the widgets that displays the currency prices might lag a bit causing inconveniences from time to time.

However, professionals claim that a simple force closing of the application is enough to rectify the problems within no time. Above all, this app is free for all the users with no extra charge for additional features making it convenient for the new investors in this online business.

f. The BlockFolio

This most common portfolio management tool provides support for both the Bitcoin and the altcoins that exist currently. You are able to monitor your various investments throughout the entire process.

This tool gives you the opportunity to access both the comprehensive overview of your portfolio and the exchanges on the particular coins trade. In addition to the outstanding features that this option provides, includes the news section.

The detailed price notifications make it easy for you to explore the various altcoins before opting to invest in them. The notification is critical following the regular wild fluctuation of the various prices.

This tool contains the order book, stock charts as well as the market details for all the currencies that are trending globally making it the one of the best consideration for the ambitious entrepreneurs, including you.

With regard to all the important features explained about this tool, I would advise you to consider the

BlockFolio as one of the powerful solutions for an improved experience with the business.

g. The 3Commas

The professionals argue that the 3Commas is one of the most complete trading tools that are available on the market for the cryptocurrencies. With this apparatus, you are able to minimize the risks while maximizing on the profits.

This platform launched back in 2017 requires you first to register after which you are entitled to enjoy a bonus of $10. Upon registering, you will be able to deal with the cryptocurrency exchanges that are currently trending, including the Binance, Poloniex, Bittrex, Kucoin as well as the Bitfinex.

This platform uses the API to connect to the cryptocurrencies you consider your favorite. However, setting this API key requires you to disable the withdrawals to keep your funds safe from fraudulent acts.

The Smart Trading property allows the investors to use the both the Stop Loss and Take Profit to enable them maximize on the profits while minimizing on the losses they are exposed to.

The StopLoss is set when the prices of the coins fall below the standardized price while the TakeProfit tool automatically closes when you have achieved your set targets in terms of profits gained. Therefore, it is recommended for you to consider this tool to enhance your cryptocurrency business endeavor.

Other than the unique tools that have been stated above, the economists advise the investors to use the trending coins like the Bitcoin or the Ethereum to get the funds to purchase the other coins that are crowding the universe.

The Coinbase and the Coinhouse are the two fastest accounts that would ensure you get your coins on time with the dream of purchasing all the coins available in the market.

Before making your conclusion, the Altcoin subredditis, YouTube channels, r/cryptocurrency, Crypto-traders Twitter accounts, CoinMonsta as well as the CoinMarketCap provide you with all the vital information before opting to purchase some of these coins. You, therefore, need to conduct comprehensive research to determine the tools that would take you to the edge in the market depending on your preference.

CHAPTER SEVEN:

Buying Cryptocurrencies

Having gone through the content of this book triggers your interest to try your luck in investing in the various altcoins that are available in the market. However, you are not able to enjoy the experience without knowing where or rather how to buy the cryptocurrencies depending on your need for the investments.

Many media exist so you can buy your coin. Fortunately, the persons with the bank account holders feeling the convenience of this process to acquire their products. A direct wire transfer occurs that allows them to buy the coins with cash using either a credit or debit card, PayPal as well as the swap cryptocurrency.

In case you have no cash to purchase the coins, you can as well work to earn the coins as payment. With regard to this, therefore, the market provides many creative ways to turn the fiat currency into crypto. On the same note, one of the sites offers to trade gifts cards for the Bitcoin, for example.

However, before purchasing the cryptocurrency ensure that you first have a wallet to help in storing your tokens. In case you are a cryptocurrency holder and you lack the wallets, you risk being a victim of hacking as well as losing much of your hard-earned cash. Therefore, the following options are important to allow you to acquire the cryptocurrencies of your choice:

I. **The Bitcoin ATM**

The Bitcoin ATMs are becoming popular worldwide. This method calls requires you to present yourself physically at the physical location to be able to complete the transaction. These machines are also convenient in case you need to purchase the altcoins. Most of these systems accepts the paper cash before serving you with a digital token in exchange.

Therefore, the Coin ATM Rader provides you with a comprehensive list and map of all the ATMs worldwide. Unfortunately, the people in the rural areas cannot access the ATMs since most of them are located in big cities.

A Bitcoin ATM

II. Buy.Cointelegraph

The Cointelegraph collaborated recently with the Simplex to allow the crypto investors to buy the alternative cryptocurrencies such as the Bitcoin Cash, Ethereum and Bitcoin with convenience.

Simplex accepts credits cards, including Mastercard and Visa as well as the debit cards and the prepaid cards.

buy.cointelegraph.com

III. The Local Bitcoins

In case there are no cryptocurrency ATMs within your region, you can consider the LocalBitcoin.com to help you locate a person who is willing to transact the cryptocurrency. This method is helpful, especially for those who like travelling internationally or those that cannot access the crypto services.

IV. Coinbase

This is the most popular service that allows the buying and selling of the cryptocurrencies such as the

Bitcoin, Litecoin and the Ethereum. The service is spread across the globe with a dozen of countries having access to the services. In United States, all the states except Wyoming, Minnesota and Hawaii have access to the experience.

You first need to download the Coinbase app on your device or rather create an account from the official website (coinbase.com) before beginning to purchase your desired coins. Upon agreeing to the terms and conditions, a chart showing the recent rise and fall of the cryptocurrencies.

From this point, you will need to add the way you would like to make your purchase. This is done by tapping the **Buy** button displayed on the app or rather a simple click on the **Buy/Sell tab** on the website.

From this point, you will need to connect either your debit or credit card for the quick and small investments. Alternatively, you can add a direct line to your personal bank account in case of the larger purchases that takes up to 5 business days to process.

Hit the **Buy** button once again then select the coin you desire purchase followed by the amount you desire to spend in U.S. Dollars. The total cost, including the small fee from the Coinbase, will display. Confirm the process by tapping the **Buy** button ones again.

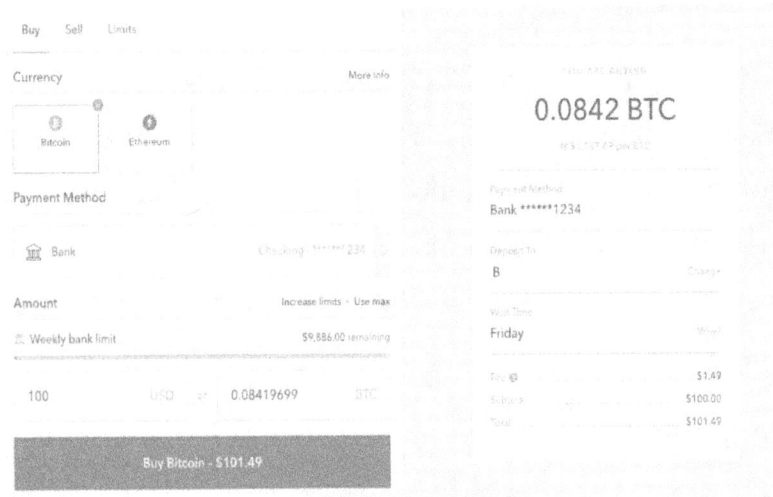

Using the Coinbase Exchange Company to purchase the coins

V. Bitfinex

This tool is another that has been in existence since 2012 to help in the purchasing the cryptocurrencies. This website boasts being the most advanced platform to trade the digital coins, with many advanced charting options during the transaction.

There is an app for both the Android and iPhone to allow you access the services at your comfort. The Exchange trading, Margin funding and the Margin trading are the three exchange features that promotes its reliability.

The integration of the P2P financing market into Bitfinex matches both the lenders and the borrowers to bring the advanced tools of margin trading. The best thing with this media is the provision of the beginners guide to ensure you get the best out of your experience.

In general

There are many different exchange media to allow you acquire your preferred coins for memorable investment experience in this online endeavor.

Why You Should Not Purchase Cryptocurrencies

Although investing in the cryptocurrency allows the crypto investors to make a fortune, they are as well exposed to risks. With regard to this, the long-term investors have identified the following as some of the reasons that discourage the new users from investing in the gold coins:

> **The growth of your investment is speculative**

Unlike in the case of the traditional companies in which the growth of your investment depends on the company's growth, turnover, earning among other external and internal factors, the prices of the respective coins depend on their demand and supply. It is, therefore, difficult to determine your success rate following your investing in the gold coins.

> **The remittance issue**

Most of the people especially consider buying the coins out of curiosity rather than as a tool of transacting. In Indi, for example, the Reserve Bank of India is warning the people against investing in the cryptocurrencies and have declared that they are not regulating the industry. There are no tangible assets to be traded with the gold coins in most of the global counties like India.

> **Your money goes down as the exchange goes down**

The fact that most of the global governments fail to associate themselves with the fraudulent bitcoin exchange, it becomes risky for the people to involve themselves in it. In case you become a victim of fraud or hacking, you lose your money. In short, you risk engaging in the buying and selling of the coins.

> **The banks have stopped the purchase of cryptocurrencies with their cards**

The Citibank, for example, notified its clients through emails that they could no longer use their debit and credit cards to purchase the gold coins. Since then, other financial institutions like the SBI Card, the second largest bank in India, spread the news regarding the risk associated with investing in the cryptocurrencies. The other banks and financial institutions have taken the same step hence discouraging new investors to try this medium of making a fortune.

> **Not all the coins will give you high returns.**

There are the self-imposed limits for each cryptocurrency on the maximum units it issues. The limiting features hinders the ambitious investors from making huge returns. You, therefore, need to be well informed before gambling with the digital coins.

Conclusion

The cryptocurrency market has flourished a decade barely after its introduction, with the ambitious investors opting to try their luck in making a fortune by investing in the digital coins.

Although the Bitcoin was the first gold coin to be transacted, there are a number of alternative cryptocurrencies that are available for trading on the cryptocurrency exchanges hence contributing to the success of these digital transactions.

Some of the popular cryptocurrencies, include the Ethereum, Litecoin, the Ripple and the original Bitcoin. The many options provide the investors with a chance to select the best coin hey feel will give them the opportunities to multiply their hard-earned cash.

Creating a crypto portfolio is the first step that the investor need to consider after deciding the amount of money they are willing to risk in this business. During this time, the investor need to decide on the specific coins they desire to risk their resources.

However, before opting to enjoy their investment, the risk takers need to have a cryptocurrency wallet to record the transaction for easy determination of the profits or loses they are exposed to.

Other than the digital wallets, there are different tools available to help in the management of the investors' portfolio to determine whether they are making profit or losses in the process. For this reason, there are many different tools available to be downloaded and installed to help in the management process. The diverse users decide on the app they think would help them realize their goals.

Despite having all this information, you need to be sure of the exchanges where you can acquire the cryptocurrencies of your choice. Ranging from the use of cash to cashless systems, there are different media from where you can purchase the coins to invest in.

Unfortunately, some of the findings by the economic analysts that discourages the global population from investing in the cryptocurrencies. It is, therefore, critical for you to conduct prior research to determine the specific coins to invest in as well as the favorable exchanges to trade them to minimize the risks and maximize on the profits.

Other Books by Ben Alexi

www.ingramcontent.com/pod-product-compliance
Lightning Source LLC
Chambersburg PA
CBHW052335220526
45472CB00001B/434